The Joy of Christmas

THE JOY

OF

CHRISTMAS

Moody Press
Chicago

*B*ut the angel said to them, 'Do not be afraid. I
bring you good news of great joy that will be
for all the people. Today in the town of David a
Savior has been born to you.'

Luke 2:10-11

Contents

The Birth of Jesus Foretold

The birth of Jesus is the sunrise of
the Bible. Towards this point the aspi-
rations of the prophets and the poems
of the psalmists were directed as the
heads of flowers are turned toward the
dawn. From this point a new day
began to flow very silently over the
world—a day of faith and freedom, a
day of hope and love. When we
remember the high
meaning that has come into human life
and the clear light that has
flooded softly down from the manger-
cradle in Bethlehem of Judea, we do
not wonder that mankind has learned
to reckon
history from the birthday of Jesus, and
to date all events by the
years before or after the
Nativity of Christ.
Henry van Dyke

*F*or to us a child is born,
to us a son is given,
and the government will be on his
  shoulders.
And he will be called
Wonderful Counselor, Mighty God,
Everlasting Father, Prince of Peace. Of the
increase of his government and
peace there will be no end. He will
reign on David's throne
and over his kingdom,
establishing it and upholding it
with justice and righteousness
from that time on and for ever.
The zeal of the LORD Almighty
will accomplish this.

Isaiah 9:6–7

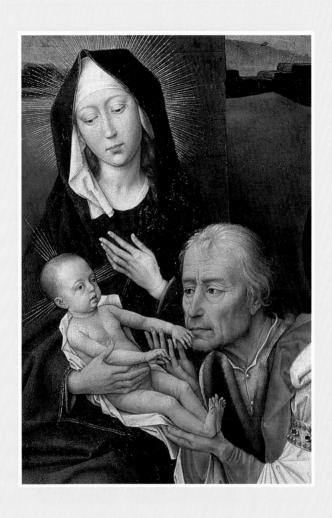

The gift-giving tradition we are familiar with today owes perhaps the most to Victorian England. The Victorians brought a renewed warmth and spirit to Christmas after it had experienced a long period of decline. They made the idea of family (and particularly children) an integral part of the celebration. They also focused on helping the less fortunate. Friendliness and charity filled many hearts during their Christmas season, so giving gifts was natural to them.

To perceive Christmas through its wrapping becomes more difficult with every year.
Elwyn B. White

Literally translated, the word "advent" means "coming." Advent is a time to reflect on the coming of Christ to earth as well as anticipate His Second Coming, to "make ready the way of the Lord." The next time you are asked, "Are you ready for Christmas?" remember that being ready has little to do with accomplishing everything on our "to-do" list. So set down those packages and that tangled string of Christmas lights. Reflect on the wonder of the incarnation, remember that the tiny baby who entered the world so quietly on that first Christmas Day will one day come again. What a good reason for Christmas!

Joseph Stowell

They were all looking for a King
To slay their foes and lift them high;
Thou cam'st a little baby thing
That made a woman cry.

George MacDonald

The Annunciation

This is how the birth of Jesus Christ came about: His mother Mary was pledged to be married to Joseph, but before they came together, she was found to be with child through the Holy Spirit. Because Joseph her husband was a righteous man and did not want to expose her to public disgrace, he had in mind to divorce her quietly.

But after he had considered this, an angel of the Lord appeared to him in a dream and said, 'Joseph, son of David, do not be afraid to take Mary home as your wife, because what is conceived in her is from the Holy Spirit. She will give birth to a son, and you are to give him the name Jesus, because he will save his people from their sins.'

All this took place to fulfill what the Lord had said through the prophet: 'The virgin will be with child and will give birth to a son, and they will call him Immanuel' — which means, 'God with us.'

When Joseph woke up, he did what the angel of the Lord had commanded him and took Mary home as his wife. But he had no union with her until she gave birth to a son. And he gave him the name Jesus.

Matthew 1:18–25

There Is Room in My Heart

Thou dids't leave Thy throne and Thy
  kingly crown,
When Thou camest to earth for me;
But in Bethlehem's home there was
found no room
For Thy holy nativity:
O come to my heart, Lord Jesus!
There is room in my heart for Thee.

Heaven's arches rang when the angels
sang,
Proclaiming Thy royal degree;
But of lowly birth cam'st Thou, Lord,
on earth,
And in great humility,
O come to my heart, Lord Jesus!
There is room in my heart for Thee.

Emily E. Steele Elliott

Somehow Not Only For Christmas

Somehow not only for Christmas
But all the long year through,
The joy that you give to others
Is the joy that comes back to you.

And the more you spend in blessing
The poor and lonely and sad,
The more of your heart's possessing
Returns to make you glad.

John Greenleaf Whittier

We pray O God that, when he comes to us, he may not find that there is no room in our hearts for him, but that this Christmas day he may enter into our hearts and live there for evermore.

William Barclay (adapted)

Words for the Magi

"Shall I bring you wisdom, shall I bring
you power?"
The first great stranger said to the child.
Then he noticed something he'd never
felt before—
A wish in himself to be innocent and mild.

"Shall I bring you glory, shall I bring
you peace?"
The second great stranger said when he
saw
The star shine down on entire helplessness.
The gift that he offered was his sense of
awe.

"Shall I show you riches?" the third one
began
Then stopped in terror because he had seen
A God grown-up and a tired tempted man.
"Suffering's my gift" he said
"That is what I mean."

Elizabeth Jennings

I Wonder as I Wander

I wonder as I wander, out under the sky,
How Jesus the Savior did come for to die
For poor or'nary people like you and
like I;
I wonder as I wander, out under the sky.

When Mary birthed Jesus, 'twas in a
cow's stall,
With wise men and farmers and shepherds and all.
But high from God's heaven a star's
light did fall,
The promise of ages it did then recall.

If Jesus had wanted for any wee thing,
A star in the sky or a bird on the wing,
Or all of God's angels in heaven for to
sing,
He surely could have it, 'cause he was
the King.

I wonder as I wander, out under the sky,
How Jesus the Savior did come for to die
For poor or'nary people like you and
like I;
I wonder as I wander, out under the sky.

Appalachian carol

Like the Shepherds

This Christmas, dear Lord,
like the shepherds,
I would bow in awed wonder
before the majesty of heaven
revealed in the form of a baby.
Fill me afresh with love
    as I contemplate the mystery.
Reveal Yourself to me so that
    like the shepherds
    and the angels
    my heart may be filled with joy.
And transform me so that
    I may become more and more like
    this Christ-child I worship:
    ready to do Your will
    in everything,
    even at cost to myself.

Joyce Huggett

Christmas

The bells of waiting Advent ring,
The tortoise stove is lit again
And lamp-oil light across the night
Has caught the streaks of winter rain
In many a stained-glass window sheen
From Crimson Lake to Hooker's Green.

The holly in the windy hedge
And round the Manor House the yew
Will soon be stripped to deck the ledge,
The altar, font and arch and pew,
So that the villagers can say
'The church looks nice' on Christmas Day.

Provincial public houses blaze
And Corporation tramcars clang,
On lighted tenements I gaze
Where paper decorations hang,
And bunting in the red Town Hall
Says 'Merry Christmas to you all.'

And London shops on Christmas Eve
Are strung with silver bells and flowers
As hurrying clerks the City leave
To pigeon-haunted classic towers,

And marbled clouds go scudding by
The many-steepled London sky.

And girls in slacks remember Dad,
And oafish louts remember Mum,
And sleepless children's hearts are
glad,
And Christmas-morning bells say
"Come!"
Even to shining ones who dwell
Safe in the Dorchester Hotel.

And is it true! And is it true,
This most tremendous tale of all,
Seen in a stained-glass window's hue,
A Baby in an ox's stall?
The Maker of the stars and sea
Become a Child on earth for me?

And is it true? For if it is,
No loving fingers tying strings
Around those tissued fripperies,
The sweet and silly Christmas things,
Bath salts and inexpensive scent
And hideous tie so kindly meant,

No love that in a family dwells,
No carolling in frosty air,
Nor all the steeple-shaking bells
Can with this single Truth compare—
That God was Man in Palestine
And lives to-day in Bread and Wine
John Betjeman

Dear Lord of the ages, and king of this coming new year, as I look to You, all things seem new.

Even my worn and sometimes broken life seems transformed. I thank You especially at this season, for the new birth and the new life which follows. Give me the grace to stand firm in the midst of temptation and give me a clearer vision of You and all that You have for me to do. Then, knowing that I am yours forever, I will praise You and love You both now and forever. Amen.

Floyd Tompkins

Silent Night

The little church in the Austrian village of Oberndorf was full for the traditional Christmas Eve service. There was a special surprise item in store. The vicar, Joseph Mohr, had written a new carol for the occasion. He had given the completed manuscript to the organist in good time for him. But now organist Franz Gruber was in despair. The organ had broken down and he could not play his tune. Undeterred, the vicar suggested that he and Herr Gruber should sing their carol as a duet.

In due course, the organ was repaired and as a test-piece during repairs, Herr Gruber played his new tune. The organ-repairer was delighted with the new carol, and when he returned to his own village of Zillerthal, he sang and played it there. A glove-maker living in Zillerthal had four daughters who used to accompany their father on his glove-selling travels and give concerts in the towns and villages they visited. These girls sang Silent Night to every available audience.

So, the carol which might have lain unknown in the church cupboard at Oberndorf became a firm favorite all over Austria. Soon it was translated into other languages, and on this Christmas Eve, more than a century and a half later, it will be sung all over the world.

Mary Batchelor

Some say that ever 'gainst that season
comes
Wherein our Savior's birth is celebrated,
The bird of dawning singeth all night
long;
And then, they say, no spirit dare stir
abroad,
The nights are wholesome; then no
  planets strike,
No fairy take, nor witch hath power to
charm,
So hallow'd and so gracious is the time.

William Shakespeare

Most of the people in Jesus' day missed His birth. They were looking for a king, not a servant. They expected a king to be born in a palace to rich parents, not in a stable to the poorest of the poor. Jesus came as a lowly servant, which is good news for us because that means there is no one with whom Jesus cannot identify.

Tony Evans

Christmas Eve

Susan took the old brown leather Bible from the dresser where it lay ready for use, and laid it on the table in front of her mother, who searched among the little texts which lay within for the place.

Joshua and Tom sat up straight to listen, Susan drew her low chair to the fire, and Becky sat down in her correct place as servant at the bottom of the table.

The wind thumped at the door, so that the latch rattled, and cried sadly as it tried to get in to listen to the tale. The flames licked round the bars and held their breath as the old words dropped peacefully in the room.

'And it came to pass in those days that there went out a decree from Caesar Augustus that all the world should be taxed . . .'

Susan could scarcely keep the tears from her eyes, she was so excited by the story she knew so well. If only she had been there too, a little girl with those

shepherds, she would have seen the
Wise Men ride up on their camels,
through the gate into the yard. They carried gold and frankincense, something,
she didn't know what, something in a
blue and gold box with red stones on it.

Then Mrs. Garland put a little embroi-
dered cross in the Bible and closed its
pages reverently. She took off her specta-
cles and laid them on the table, and they
all knelt down to pray.

They prayed for the Queen and
Country, for the three doves, Peace,
Wisdom, and Understanding, and they
thanked God for all the blessings of this
life.

But Susan's head began to nod, and
she rested it on the hard chair. When the
others arose, she still knelt there, fast
asleep.

So her mother roused her, and she
said 'Good night, God bless you,' for
anyone might disappear in the night, and
they went upstairs together to the Little
Chamber, where a fire burned in

the grate, and shadows jumped up and down the ceiling, fire-shadows the best of all.

She hung up her stocking at the foot of the bed and fell asleep. But soon singing roused her, and she sat up, bewildered. Yes, it was the carol-singers.

Margaret came running upstairs and wrapped her in a blanket. She took her across the landing to her own room, and pulled up the linen blind.

Outside under the stars she could see the group of men and women with lanterns throwing beams across the paths and on to the stable door. One man stood apart beating time, another played a fiddle, and another had a flute. The rest sang in four parts the Christmas hymns, 'While shepherds watched', 'Come all ye faithful', and 'Hark, the herald angels sing'.

There was the star. Susan could see it twinkling and bright in the dark boughs with their white frosted layers, and there was the stable. She watched

the faces half lit by the lanterns, top-coats pulled up to their necks. The music of the violin came thin and squeaky, like a singing icicle, blue and cold, but magic, and the flute was warm like the voices.

They stopped and waited a moment. Tom's deep voice came from the darkness. They trooped, chattering and puffing out their cheeks, and clapping their arms round their bodies, to the front door. They were going into the parlour for elderberry wine and their collection money. A bright light flickered across the snow as the door was flung wide open. Then a bang, and Susan went back to bed.

Christmas Eve was nearly over, but tomorrow was Christmas Day, the best day in all the year. She shut her eyes and fell asleep.

Alison Uttley

O Little Town of Bethlehem

O little town of Bethlehem,
How still we see thee lie!
Above thy deep and dreamless sleep
The silent stars go by.
Yet in the dark streets shineth
The everlasting light;
The hopes and fears of all the years
Are met in Thee tonight.

Philips Brooks

Christmas comes each year to draw people in from the cold. Christmas offers its wonderful message, Emmanuel, God with us. He who resides in Heaven, co-equal and co-eternal with the Father and the Spirit, willingly descended into our world. He breathed our air, felt our pain, knew our sorrows, and died for our sins. He didn't come to frighten us, but to show us the way to warmth and safety.

Charles Swindoll

From the cradle in Bethlehem to the cross in Jerusalem we've pondered the love of our Father. What can you say to that kind of emotion? Upon learning that God would rather die than live without you, how do you react? How can you begin to explain such passion?

Max Lucado

46

The First Christmas Tree

St Boniface of Credition was born in about AD 675. He preached to the heathen tribes of Germany. The villagers of Bortharia had been suffering from storms and plague. They intended to appease the god Odin by offering him a human sacrifice. Led by their chief, they assembled in the forest clearing at midnight. The priest tied a boy — the appointed victim — to the sacred oak and prepared to kill him.

At that moment, a breathless silence was broken by a shout. Dark-clad figures of Christian monks approached the scene of sacrifice, and their leader, Boniface, called out, 'Stop, in the name of Jesus Christ!'

The villagers were terrified. What new reprisals from their god would such blasphemy bring forth? But Boniface reasoned, 'If Odin is really god, he can defend himself and prove himself. Let the boy go.'

There was no thunderbolt, no vengeance hurled at the Christian monk. The boy was untied, and Boniface began to tell the Bortharians the good news of God's love and mercy in Jesus Christ.

Then he offered them a young fir tree in place of the oak, planting it and placing his candle on it. His companions added their candles, and the fir tree shone out in the dark forest, a picture of God's ever-living love and of the light that has come into the world in Jesus Christ.

Mary Batchelor

How many observe Christ's
birthday! How few, his precepts!
O! 'tis easier to keep holidays
than commandments.
Benjamin Franklin

Christmas in the Heart

To Bethlehem our hearts, star-led
  From wanderings far and wild,
Turn to a lowly cattle-shed
  And kneel before the Child.

We come from deserts, pitiless
  With only human pride;
And from the howling wilderness
  Where dread and hate abide.

Touched by His hand we find release
  From heavy griefs and fears:
Our hearts are lifted up with peace
  And purified by tears.

Ah Saviour dear! Thou Holy Child,
  What power is thine to heal
Our broken hearts, our wills, defiled,
  When at Thy feet we kneel.

Grant us Thy grace no more to roam,
  But, following Thee alway,
Find Bethlehem in every home,
  The whole year Christmas Day.

Henry Van Dyke

A Christmas Prayer

Loving looks the large-eyed cow,
Loving stares the long-eared ass
At Heaven's glory in the grass!
Child, with added human birth
Come to bring the child of earth
Glad repentance, tearful mirth,
And a seat beside the hearth
At the Father's knee —
Make us peaceful as Thy cow;
Make us patient as Thine ass;
Make us quiet as Thou art now;
Make us strong as Thou wilt be.
Make us always know and see
We are His, as well as Thou.

George MacDonald

In the Bleak Midwinter

What can I give Him,
Poor as I am?
If I were a shepherd,
I would bring a lamb.
If I were a wise man,
I would do my part;
Yet what I can I give Him—
Give my heart.

Christina G. Rossetti

Love Came Down at Christmas

Love came down at Christmas.
Love all lovely, Love Divine;
Love was born at Christmas,
Star and angels gave the sign.

Love shall be our token,
Love be yours and love be
mine.
Love to God and all men.
Love for plea and gift and sign.

Christina G. Rossetti

The Voice of the Christ-Child

The feet of the humblest may
walk in the field
Where the feet of the holiest
have trod,
This, this is the marvel to mortals
revealed,
When the silvery trumpets of
Christmas have pealed,
That mankind are the children of God.

Phillips Brooks

Born to Raise the Sons of Earth

I am busy, Jesus,
ever faster screeching round and
round—
You lie calmly in the manger,
Joseph's patient voice the only sound.

I am selfish, Jesus,
grasping, pulling inward, curved in
tight—
You stoop lower, ever lower,
mixing spittle for a poor man's sight.

I am sated, Jesus,
stuffed so full I've almost lost my
breath—
You are rasping, breathing labored,
stumbling naked, famished to Your
death.

I am tired, Jesus,
numb and finished, callous and dis-
tressed—You stand wounded, weeping,
dying,
quickened; calling, 'Come to me and rest.'

Mark Noll

The Three Wise Men

After Jesus was born in Bethlehem in Judea, during the time of King Herod, Magi from the east came to Jerusalem and asked, 'Where is the one who has been born king of the Jews? We saw his star in the east and have come to worship him.'

When King Herod heard this he was disturbed and all Jerusalem with him. When he had called together all the people's chief priests and teachers of the law, he asked them where the Christ was to be born. 'In Bethlehem in Judea,' they replied, 'for this is what the prophet has written:

' "But you, Bethlehem, in the land of Judah, are by no means least among the rulers of Judah; for out of you will come a ruler who will be the shepherd of my people Israel." '

Then Herod called the Magi secretly and found out from them the exact time the star had appeared. He sent them to Bethlehem and said, 'Go and make a careful search for the child. As soon as you find him, report to me, so that I too may go and worship him.'

After they had heard the king, they went on their way, and the star they had seen in the east went ahead of them until it stopped over the place where the child was. When they saw the star, they were overjoyed. On coming to the house, they saw the child with his mother Mary, and they bowed down and worshipped him. Then they opened their treasures and presented him with gifts of gold and of incense and of myrrh. And having been warned in a dream not to go back to Herod, they returned to their country by another route.

Matthew 2:1–12

The Three Kings

And the three kings rode through the
gate and the guard,
Through the silent street, till their
horses turned
And neighed as they entered the great
inn-yard;
But the windows were closed, and the
doors were barred,
And only a light in the stable burned.

And cradled there in the scented hay,
In the air made sweet by the breath of
kine,
The little child in the manger lay,
The child, that would be king one day
Of a kingdom not human but divine.

His mother Mary of Nazareth
Sat watching beside his place of rest,
Watching the even flow of his breath,
For the joy of life and the terror of death
Were mingled together in her breast.

They laid their offerings at his feet:
The gold was their tribute to a King,
The francincense, with its odour sweet,
Was for the Priest, the Paraclete,
The myrrh for the body's burying.

And the mother wondered and bowed
her head,
And sat as still as a statue of stone;
Her heart was troubled yet comforted,
Remembering what the Angel had said
Of an endless reign and of David's
throne.

Henry Wadsworth Longfellow (abridged)

Merry, Merry Christmas

Christmas time! That man must be a misanthrope indeed, in whose breast something like a jovial feeling is not roused – in whose mind some pleasant associations are not awakened – by the recurrence of Christmas.

There are people who will tell you that Christmas is not to them what it used to be; that each succeeding Christmas has found some cherished hope, or happy prospect, of the year before, dimmed or passed away; that the present only serves to remind them of reduced circumstances and straitened incomes – of the feasts they once bestowed on hollow friends, and of the cold looks that meet them now, in adversity and misfortune.

Never heed such dismal reminiscences. There are few men who have lived long enough in the world, who cannot call up such thoughts any day in the year. Then do not select the merriest of the three hundred and sixty-five for your doleful recollections, but draw your chair nearer the blazing-fire – fill the glass and send round the song and if your room be smaller than it was a dozen years ago, or if your glass be filled with reeking punch, instead of sparkling wine, put a good face on the matter, and empty it off-hand, and fill another, and troll off the old ditty you used to sing, and thank God it's no worse . . .

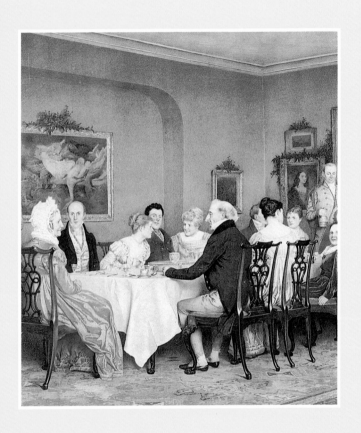

Who can be insensible to the outpourings of good feeling, and the honest interchange of affectionate attachment which abound at this season of the year.

A Christmas family-party! We know nothing in nature more delightful! There seems a magic in the very name of Christmas. Petty jealousies and discords are forgotten; social feelings are awakened, in bosoms to which they have long been strangers; father and son, or brother and sister, who have met and passed with averted gaze, or a look of cold recognition, for months before, proffer and return the cordial embrace, and bury their past animosities in their present happiness. Kind hearts that have yearned towards each other but have been withheld by false notions of pride and self-dignity, are again reunited, and all is kindness and benevolence!

Would that Christmas lasted the whole year through (as it ought) and that the prejudices and passions which deform our better nature were never called into action among those to whom they should ever be strangers!

Charles Dickens

Christmas Food and Drink

Many of today's traditional Christmas foods were customary centuries ago. The goose, for example, has been a well established part of the festive table since the middle ages. Turkey did not appear on the Christmas menu until the mid-sixteenth century, when it was imported from America. It subsequently overtook goose in popularity, however, and huge flocks of turkeys were reared in Norfolk and Suffolk, as many as today, and driven to London as Christmas drew nearer, resting and grazing on wayside verges as they travelled.

Vast Christmas pies were also made in the middle ages, containing duck, capons, pigeons, blackbirds, snipe and woodcock, and it was into this kind of pie that Little Jack Horner, steward to the Abbot of Glastonbury, reputedly put his thumb and pulled out a plumb: the deeds of twelve Somerset manors. The pie was being sent as a present from the Abbot to curry favour with the king, Henry VIII, and Jack Horner was entrusted with the task of conveying it safely to London.

Traditional Christmas food also included cakes, nuts, marzipan, gingerbread, and plum porridge, the forerunner of Christmas pudding made by boiling beef and mutton

to make a kind of thick soup containing breadcrumbs, raisins, currants, prunes, wine and spices. It was eaten with the first course of Christmas dinner.

Mince pies were eaten before they became associated with Christmas. They date back to the time of the Crusades, when England was first introduced to oriental spices. These were used to season minced meat, and often to disguise the fact that it was not as fresh as it might have been. In the seventeenth century, the Puritans banned Christmas celebrations and for a while mince pies were not seen. When they came to be made again they contained raisins, orange and lemon peel and sugar, as well as their previous ingredients. Over the years the meat content of mince pies disappeared, and is represented today only by the inclusion of suet.

The traditional English Christmas drink was wassail, so-called from the Saxon greeting 'waes hael' ('be well'). It was made from heated ale, roast apples, eggs, sugar and spices, and was carried from household to household in a wooden bowl. Most families kept a pan of wassail warming on the hearth, from which they would refill the bowls of those who called on them.

Josceline Dimbleby

Keeping Christmas

He who regards one day as special,
does so to the Lord.
Romans 14:6

It is a good thing to observe Christmas day. The mere marking of times and seasons, when men agree to stop work and make merry together, is a wise and wholesome custom. It reminds a man to set his own little watch, now and then, by the great clock of humanity.

But there is a better thing than the observance of Christmas day, and that is, keeping Christmas.

Are you willing to forget what you have done for other people, and to remember what other people have done for you; to ignore what the world owes you, and to think what you owe the world; to put your rights in the background, and your duties in the middle distance, and your chances to do a little more than your duty in the foreground; to see that your fellow-men are just as real as you are, and try to look behind their faces to their hearts, hungry for joy; to admit that probably the only good reason for your existence is not what you are going to get out of life, but what you are going to give to life; to close your

book of complaints against the management of the universe, and look around you for a place where you can sow a few seeds of happiness — are you willing to do all this for a day? Then you can keep Christmas.

Are you willing to stoop down and consider the needs and the desires of little children; to remember the weakness and loneliness of people who are growing old; to stop asking how much your friends love you, and ask yourself whether you love them enough; to try to understand what those who live in the same house with you really want, without waiting for them to tell you; to make a grave for your ugly thoughts, and a garden for your kindly feelings, with the gate open – are you willing to do these things even for a day? Then you can keep Christmas. Are you willing to believe that love is the strongest thing in the world — stronger than hate, evil, and death — and that the blessed life which began in Bethlehem nineteen hundred years ago is the image and brightness of the Eternal Love?

Then you can keep Christmas. And if you can keep it for a day, why not always?

But you can never keep it alone.

Henry Van Dyke

'Twas the night before Christmas, when
all through the house
Not a creature was stirring, not even a
mouse;
The stockings were hung by the chimney
with care,
In hopes that St Nicholas soon would
be there.

Professor Clement C. Moore

The best Christmas gift of all is
the presence of a happy
family all wrapped up with
one another.
E. C. McKenzie

PRAYERS.

A Merry Christmas

A Christmas Prayer

In the morning

O God our Father, we thank You for Christmas, and all that it means to us.

We thank you that when Your Son Jesus came into this world He came into a humble home.

We thank You that He had to grow up and to learn just like any other boy.

We thank You that He did a good day's work, when He grew to manhood, as the carpenter in the village shop in Nazareth.

We thank You that He was tempted and tired, hungry and sad, just as we are.

We thank You that He was one with His brothers in all things, that He truly shared this life with its struggles and its toils, its sorrows and its joys, its trials and its temptations.

We thank You that He knew what it is to live in a home circle, just as we do; to earn His living, just as we do; to know friendship and to know the failure of friends, just as we know it.

We thank You for the service of His life; the love of His death; and the power of His resurrection. Amen

In the evening

O God our Father, we thank You for the happiness of this Christmas Day.

For the presents we have received; for the happiness we have enjoyed; for the meals we have eaten together, the games we have played together, the talk we have had together. We thank You Lord.

We thank You for the peace and good will which have been amongst us all today. May they not be something which lasts only for today, but we pray we might take the Christmas joy and the Christmas fellowship with us into all the ordinary days of life.

We especially remember those for whom this Christmas has not been a happy time. Bless those to whom sorrow came, and for whom it was all the more painful because it came at a time when everyone else was so happy. Bless those who have no friends, no homes, no family, no one to remember them. Be with them in their loneliness to comfort and cheer them. O God we thank You for today; help us to try to deserve our happiness a little more. Through Jesus Christ our Lord. Amen

William Barclay (adapted)

Text Credits

Care has been taken to attribute all quotes from all sources, and to clear all permissions. We are grateful to the following for their permission and apologise for any unintentional omissions. The full works of the Moody Press authors quoted is also listed.

Barclay, William, pp 21, 80, 82: *The Plain Man's Book of Prayers* (London: Fontana, 1968).

Batchelor, Mary, pp 32, 47: *The Everyday Book* (Oxford: Lion Publishing, 1982).

Betjeman, John, p 28: *Christmas* (Curtis Brown Ltd).

Dimbleby, Josceline, p 70: *The Josceline Dimbleby Christmas Book* (London: Woodhead Faulkner Publishers Ltd. for J. Sainsbury plc, 1987).

Evans, Tony, p 35: works published by Moody Press: *Who Is This King of Glory?: Experiencing The Fullness of Christ's Work in Our Lives*, 1999; *The Battle Is the Lord's: Waging Victorious Spiritual Warfare*, 1998; *What Matters Most: Four Absolute Necessities in Following Christ*, 1997; *Returning to Your First Love: Putting God Back in First Place*, 1995; *The Promise: Experiencing God's Greatest Gift*, 1996; *Our God is Awesome: Encountering the Greatness of Our God*, 1994; *Are Christians Destroying America?: How to Restore a Decaying Culture*, 1996; *Tony Evans Speaks Out On Divorce and Remarriage*, 1995; *Tony Evans Speaks Out On Gambling and the Lottery*, 1995; *Tony Evans Speaks Out On Sexual Purity*, 1995; *Tony Evans Speaks Out On Single Parenting*, 1995.

Huggett, Joyce, p 26: *Embracing God's World* (London: Hodder & Stoughton, 1996).

Jennings, Elizabeth, p 23, source not found.

Longfellow, Henry Wadsworth, p 63: *The Three Kings*, from *Consequently I Rejoice* (Carcanet Press – David Higham Associates).

Lucado, Max, p 45: *In the Grip of Grace* (Nashville, TN, Word Publishing, 1996).

MacDonald, George, pp 14, 52: quoted in Henry van Dyke, *A Treasury of Christmas Stories* (Wheaton, Ill.: Harold Shaw Publishers, 1993).

Stowell, Joseph, p 14: works published by Moody Press: *Kingdom Conflict: Personal Triumph in a Supernatural Struggle*, Revised and Expanded edition 1996; *Far from Home: The Soul's Search for Intimacy with God*, 1998; *The Weight of Your Words: Measuring the Impact of What You Say*, 1998; *Perilous Pursuits: Our Obsession with Significance*, 1994; *Eternity: Reclaiming a Passion for What Endures*, 1997; *Loving Those We'd Rather Hate: Developing Compassion in an Angry World*, 1994; *Overcoming Evil with Good:*

The Impact of a Life Well-Lived, 1995; *The Upside of Down: Finding Hope When It Hurts*, 1991; *Shepherding the Church: Effective Spiritual Ledership in a Changing Culture*, 1997.

Swindoll, Charles, p 45: *The Finishing Touch* (Nashville, TN, Word Publishing, 1994).

Uttley, Alison, pp 37-42: *Country World* (London: Faber & Faber, 1984).

van Dyke, Henry, pp 9, 51, 74: *A Treasury of Christmas Stories* (Wheaton, Ill.: Harold Shaw Publishers, 1993).

Picture Credits

The following abbreviations are used throughout:BAL: Bridgeman Art Library, London; FAPL: Fine Art Photographic Library Ltd., London.

p 5   Rembrandt van Rijn, 1606–1669; *The annunciation of the angel Gabriel to Mary.* Besançon, Musée des Beaux-Arts.

p 8   Rembrandt van Rijn, 1606–1669; *The Shepherds Worship the Child.* London, National Gallery.

p 11   Rogier van der Weyden, 1400–1464; *The Adoration of the Magi* (detail). c.1455. BAL/Munich, Alte Pinakothek.

p 12   Albert Chevallier Tayler, 1862–1925; *The Christmas Tree.* BAL/Private Collection.

p 15   Friederich Ortlieb, 1839–1909; *A Christmas Recital.* FAPL.

p 17   Fra Angelico, 14th century; *The Annunciation.* Florence, San Marco Convent.

p 19   Flemish School (early 16th century); *Adoration of the Child.* Fitzwilliam Museum, Cambridge.

p 20   Arthur Joseph Gaskin, 1862–1928; *The Nativity,* 1925. FAPL.

p 22   Hans Acker, 15th century; *The nativity.* Ulm Cathedral, Germany.

p 24   Anon, 19th century; *Carol Singing.* FAPL.

p 27   Thomas Sidney Cooper, 1803–1902, *Winter,* 1861. FAPL.

p 29   George Sheridan Knowles, 1863–1931; *Christmas.* FAPL.

p 33   Smith-Hald Frithjof, 1846–1903; *Winter Sports.* FAPL/Baumkotter Gallery.

p 34   Hermann Kauffmann, 1808–1889; *The Timber Wagon.* FAPL/Colin Stodgell.

p 36   Albert Chevallier Tayler, 1862–1925; *The Christmas Tree* (detail). See p 12.

p 38   French(?) School; *The Three Magi (detail),* The Wilton Diptych. London, National Gallery.

p 41   Walter Anderson, fl. 1856–86; *Christmas Eve.* FAPL/Private Collection.

p 43   Louis van Engelen, 1856–1940; *Christmas Visitors.* FAPL/Galerie Berko.

p 44   Fra Angelico, *Angel with drum.* Florence, San Marco Convent. Scala.

p 46   Anon; *Christmas in Moscow,* 1941. BAL/Private Collection.

p 48   Johansen, Viggo, 1851-1935; *Happy Christmas* (detail). BAL/Hirsch Sprungske, Copenhagen.

p 50   Tres Belles Heures du Duc de Berry, begun c.1382. *Nativity and visitation of the Shepherds.* BAL/Paris, Bibliotheque Nationale.

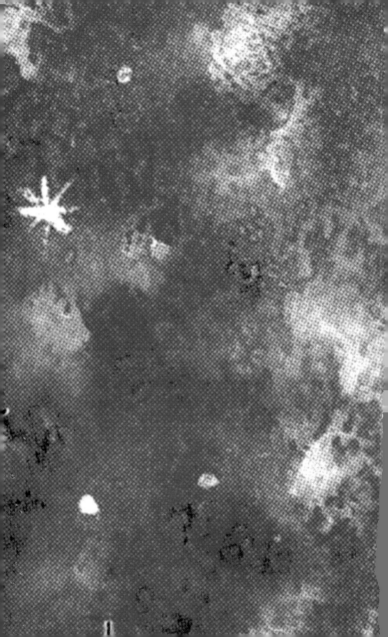